The Seasonal Visitor

Further titles in this series

A Busker on Bow Street

Lost Dreams

The Farmer's Son

The Seasonal Visitor

Short Stories for Adult Learners No. 4

LinguaBooks Readers

Published in the United Kingdom by LinguaBooks

ISBN: 978-1-911369-13-4

A CIP catalogue record for this book is available from the British Library.

Series editor: Maurice Claypole
Edited by: Ann Claypole
Proofreader: Marie-Christin Strobel

LinguaBooks
Elsie Whiteley Innovation Centre
Hopwood Lane, Halifax HX1 5ER
www.linguabooks.com

The world is shaped by two things – stories told and the memories they leave behind.

– Vera Nazarian

ACKNOWLEDGEMENTS

Some of these stories first appeared in *The Written Word*, a journal for English-speaking residents of Baden-Württemberg, Germany.

The publishers would like to thank the authors of the original stories for offering their work for publication and similarly to express their gratitude to all who were involved in producing both *The Written Word* and the present collection, thereby enabling these stories to reach a wider audience within the context of adult literacy and language learning.

Image credits: cover, page 9, 18, 30, 39, 40, 51 Dreamstime; 17, 123RF, pixabay, tabletmag.com, coloringgames.com; 29 Vecteezy, 50 Vectorstock, Canstockphoto, pixabay; 64 FreeArt, Alamy, LinguaBooks, pixabay

Contents

Introduction

This LinguaBooks Reader is the fourth volume of short stories to be published in this innovative new series.

The stories are presented as originally written by native speakers of English from a variety of countries and backgrounds. Although the punctuation and spelling have largely been harmonised, no attempt has been made to simplify or sanitise the language used. The main objective here is to give learners and other readers an authentic language experience whilst at the same time providing plenty of scope for language acquisition, enhanced awareness and vocabulary expansion. From a point of view of difficulty, the language varies in terms of complexity and register and may be considered equivalent to Level C1 of the Common European Framework of Reference for Languages (CEFR).

The content and scope make each book in this series ideal for classroom use, but the stories can also be read for pleasure, with or without recourse to the supplementary material included. The words and phrases explained after each story provide useful assistance, but lay no claim to completeness, since learners nowadays have ready access to a wide range of external resources. Autonomous learners who favour an active approach will also benefit from the activities and puzzles, which represent a combination of consolidation and discovery exercises. An answer key is provided for the convenience of learners, teachers and independent readers.

The Seasonal Visitor

by Maurice Claypole

— ❧ ❧ —

The fire in the hearth was burning low as the silent whisper of a chill wind hissed through the cracks in the windowpanes. The snow on the gloomy hills muffled all sounds from outside; only the ticking of the clock on the mantelpiece disturbed the silence. A glance told Gwyneth that it was one minute to twelve – sixty seconds to the end of what had not been a good year.

Images flashed through her mind – the accident, the hospital, the solemn procession through the churchyard and the final farewell. At first, people had been understanding, supportive, consoling her for her loss, but slowly the harsh realities of life had begun to pile up. The promise to keep her job open had come to nothing when the advertising agency had been taken over. She had even been turned away by the new supermarket looking for part-time staff. The initial flow of understanding letters from relatives and friends had faded away, leaving only a mounting pile of bills and final demands. The unopened newspaper lay on the floor where she had discarded it yesterday. What was the point in even looking at the situations vacant any more? No-one wanted a burned-out graphic designer.

The minute hand on the clock joined the hour hand at the top of the dial. The fire flickered a little and seemed to go dark for a moment as the icy wind increased its pitch to a high whine before fading away completely. Then the room seemed to become warmer, lighter, as though caught in the glow of a giant candle.

At first, she did not see him standing by the mantelpiece, and when she did she was too overcome by surprise to utter a word. A deep intake of breath as joy mixed with fear left her speechless, mouth gaping. It was as if she could both see Daniel and see through him at the same time, but then this vapid quality seemed to vanish as he moved towards her.

When she found her voice it was little more than a whimper, "Is it really you?"

Daniel smiled, took her hands, gently pulling her to her feet.

"Hello, honey," he said, "I'm here to give you your strength back."

It was the old familiar lilt, the sparkle in the eyes that she thought she had lost forever.

"Oh, Daniel," she sobbed as she fell into his arms.

"Hush," he said gently stroking her cheek, "let's not waste time. They only let me do this once a year."

Together they drifted towards the staircase ...

When she awoke the next morning, it was as if all the songbirds of spring were outside her window. Pulling the curtains apart, she looked out over the winter landscape and tore open the window. A sudden breeze caused something on the floor to flutter at the corner of her eye – the newspaper. It was open at the jobs page and one of the announcements was ringed in red ink. 'Graphic Designer needed urgently. Excellent pay and prospects.' In the margin was a handwritten note 'Try this. Tell me all about it next year.' The handwriting was Daniel's.

— తు ♋ —

Words and phrases

windowpanes	glass parts of windows
gloomy	dark, dismal, dreary
muffled	quietened, deadened
mantelpiece	shelf above a fireplace
consoling	comforting
harsh	hard, bitter
come to nothing	failed
taken over	Bought, e.g. by another company, acquired
mounting pile	increasing number
final demands	last requests for payment before legal action
situations vacant	job advertisements
utter	speak
fading away	getting weaker
mouth gaping	mouth wide open
vapid	lacking form, not lifelike
found her voice	was able to speak
whimper	low, broken, sobbing sound
lilt	lively rhythm of speech
at the corner of her eye	on the edge of her vision
urgently	immediately
prospects	financial expectations, chances of promotion

Food for thought

1. On which day of the year does the story begin?
   a. on New Year's Eve
   b. on Christmas Eve
   c. on the anniversary of an accident

2. *'The final farewell'* What does this refer to?
   a. the last time she saw someone
   b. a funeral service
   c. her last day at work

3. Why had she not opened the newspaper?
   a. The news wasn't worth reading any more.
   b. She hadn't had time to read it.
   c. She had given up hope of finding a new job.

4. What happened when Daniel moved towards her?
   a. She could hear him breathing.
   b. He seemed to become more lifelike.
   c. She reached out to touch him.

5. Which word best characterises the end of the story?
   a. hope
   b. ambition
   c. resignation

Crossword puzzle

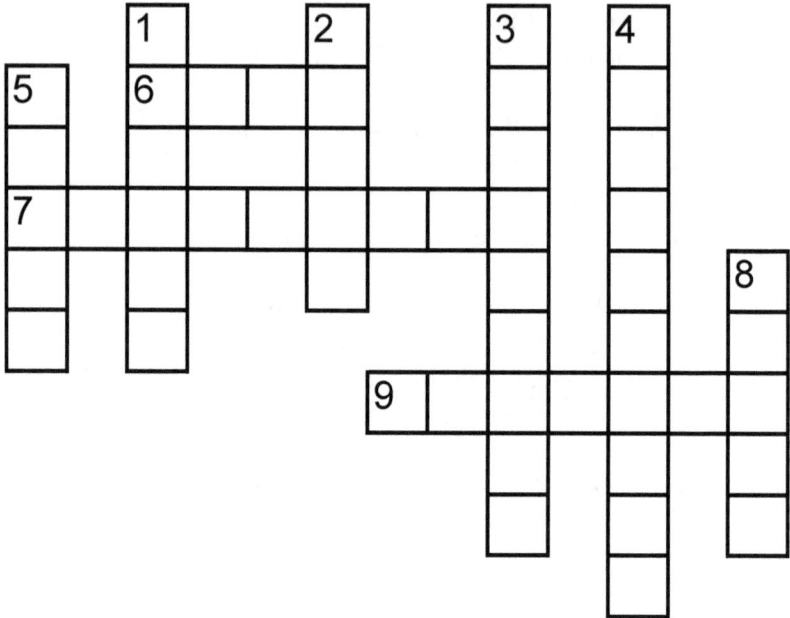

ACROSS

6 lively speech rhythm

7 chances of promotion

9 low sobbing sound

DOWN

1 dismal

2 speak

3 comforting

4 glass of a window

5 lacking form

8 bitter

Picture quiz – seasonal festivals

A Name the festivals illustrated below. Use the initial letters given.

1   2   3

4   5   6

1 C_____   **2** H_____   **3** E_____

4 H_____   **5** N_____   **6** D_____

B Match the festivals above with the words below.
1 hunt ( ) **2** chime ( ) **3** menorah ( )
4 diya ( ) **5** Jack-o'-lantern ( ) **6** mistletoe ( )

A Scarecrow in Winter

by Anthony Curtis

— ❧ ❧ —

Mist swirled lightly in the woods, stirred by a cold breeze between the trees. Through the mist a man appeared. A woollen balaclava covered most of his head and face. Only his eyes were visible; eyes which stared directly ahead, showing no apparent interest in their surroundings. His arms hung down to his sides, only now and then did he use them to push aside branches, He wore a thick overcoat, which reached almost down to his ankles, and on his feet were sturdy leather boots.

Making his way slowly through the woods, he eventually came to a large clearing. The mist did not allow him to see how large it was, but from the furrows on which he now stood, he judged it to be a ploughed field. He walked along its perimeter and suddenly stopped. Through the mist a vague shadow could be seen. The man thought at first that it was a tree, but decided that it was too symmetrical, it looked rather like a cross. Intrigued, he trod carefully over the muddy, uneven ground towards it. As he came nearer, he recognised the object and laughed out loud.

With a bow and a mock flourish of the hand he said, "Why good morning, Mr Scarecrow, fancy meeting you here!"

The man surveyed the scarecrow with a critical eye. His head was a large pumpkin with slits for eyes and mouth, adorned with an old hat and impaled on a vertical wooden cross. A tattered shirt and dungarees filled with straw concealed the scarecrow's skeletal figure. Straw protruded from the extremities of the slats where his hands and feet should have been. The man plucked nervously at a piece of straw which stuck out of the shirt, then jumped back in alarm as a tiny field mouse appeared from one of the pockets of the dungarees. For a nanosecond in eternity, man and mouse stared at each other; then the mouse sprang to the ground and scurried away.

"Well!" exclaimed the man. "That was most unexpected. Have you got any more surprises for me?"

He shook the post gently, but there was no further activity.

There followed a short silence, then the man said, "You're probably wondering what I'm doing here. Well, I'll tell you. I came here to get away from it all."

He stood staring at his gloves, as if giving the scarecrow time to digest this information.

"You don't believe me," he stated at length. "Well, I'm here, and I'll wager that I'm the only person crazy enough to traverse the woods at such an early hour. It's cold and it's damp, and I don't suppose anyone would care if I caught pneumonia or something, but I should worry."

He flung out his arms. A gesture of despair.

"She left me, you know. And my kids were sent off to New Zealand to their grandparents. Hers, not mine. That's what hurts most. They took her side. Said I never had time for the family - always working. But I ask you, Mr Scarecrow, what else could I do? They couldn't appreciate that it was all for them. A house in the country with all the latest gadgets, everything for their comfort. An ultra-modern dwelling, with solar power to boot.

"If you could walk, Mr Scarecrow, I'd take you there. It's not very far from here. Oh, how the roof sparkles in the sunlight. There's nothing like it for miles around, and the neighbours look at it with envy. But now it's empty, even when I'm there. What's the use of having a large house if there's only one person to live in it? Might as well take a bedsitter. Yes, that's what I'll do. Sell the house. Don't you worry. I'm not too old to start afresh somewhere else."

The harsh cry of a crow interrupted the man who automatically looked upwards, but the mist hung heavily over the field, and he could only see the scarecrow and the soil beneath his feet.

"You know something, Mr Scarecrow? I like you. I can talk to you without the fear of being argued with. It's time someone heard my point of view. Oh, I can't say that I'm always right, but then again, I can't always be wrong, can I? You understand me, don't you?"

The scarecrow made no reply.

The man suddenly grasped the post on which it hung and shook it violently.

Faint rustlings of falling straw.

"Oh, what's the use," growled the man. "You're only a scarecrow, what would you know about anything?"

Then he turned his back on the dilapidated figure, walked towards the woods, and disappeared in the mist.

After a while, the silence he left behind was broken by a flapping of invisible wings, but the unrelenting scarecrow stood with its head hanging down on its chest, apparently not giving a damn about anything.

— ❧ ☙ —

Words and phrases

balaclava	hat that covers the head and neck with an opening for the eyes or face
furrows	long shallow trenches in the ground made by a plough
ploughed field	fields with furrows ready for sowing
perimeter	outer edge of an area
flourish	sweeping movement
scarecrow	man-shaped object, designed to frighten away birds
Fancy meeting...!	What a surprise to meet...!
dungarees	a type of working trousers
digest	process
wager	bet
traverse	cross
gesture	bodily expression
gadgets	devices, appliances
to boot	as well, also
might as well...	probably better to...
grasped	held firmly, gripped
dilapidated	broken, shabby, neglected
flapping	moving up and down
unrelenting	merciless, without pity

Food for thought

1. *'With a bow and a mock flourish of the hand.'* What does this action indicate?
    a. an exaggerated traditional greeting
    b. a gesture of surprise
    c. a sign of desperation

2. Why does the narrator fling out his arms in despair?
    a. Because the scarecrow is not listening.
    b. He wishes he were back in his nice country house.
    c. He is upset because his wife has left him.

3. Which sentence best summarises the man's attitude when he talks about his house?
    a. He feels trapped in the past.
    b. He wants to start a new life.
    c. He is resigned to his fate.

4. Why does the man suddenly shake the scarecrow?
    a. To give vent to his emotions.
    b. Because he heard something move in the straw.
    c. He wants to know if the scarecrow is alive.

5. Which word best describes the man's attitude at the end of the story?
    a. reassured
    b. determined
    c. frustrated

Word search

Find the words in the grid. Words can go horizontally, vertically or diagonally in any direction.

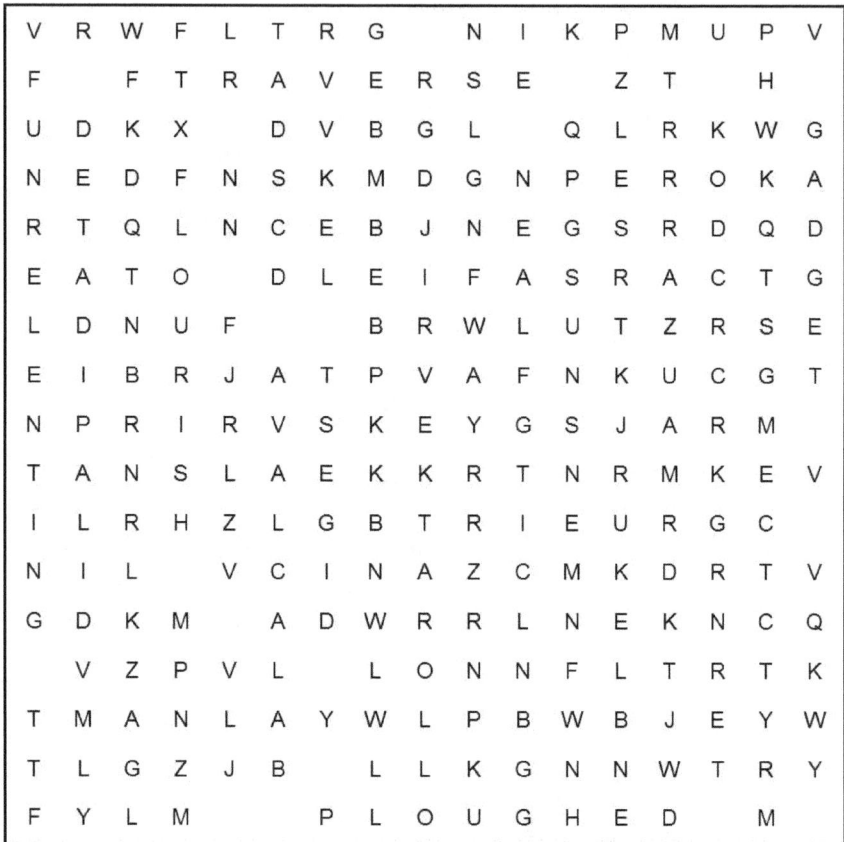

V	R	W	F	L	T	R	G		N	I	K	P	M	U	P	V
F		F	T	R	A	V	E	R	S	E		Z	T		H	
U	D	K	X		D	V	B	G	L		Q	L	R	K	W	G
N	E	D	F	N	S	K	M	D	G	N	P	E	R	O	K	A
R	T	Q	L	N	C	E	B	J	N	E	G	S	R	D	Q	D
E	A	T	O		D	L	E	I	F	A	S	R	A	C	T	G
L	D	N	U	F			B	R	W	L	U	T	Z	R	S	E
E	I	B	R	J	A	T	P	V	A	F	N	K	U	C	G	T
N	P	R	I	R	V	S	K	E	Y	G	S	J	A	R	M	
T	A	N	S	L	A	E	K	K	R	T	N	R	M	K	E	V
I	L	R	H	Z	L	G	B	T	R	I	E	U	R	G	C	
N	I	L		V	C	I	N	A	Z	C	M	K	D	R	T	V
G	D	K	M		A	D	W	R	R	L	N	E	K	N	C	Q
	V	Z	P	V	L		L	O	N	N	F	L	T	R	T	K
T	M	A	N	L	A	Y	W	L	P	B	W	B	J	E	Y	W
T	L	G	Z	J	B		L	L	K	G	N	N	W	T	R	Y
F	Y	L	M			P	L	O	U	G	H	E	D		M	

balaclava	flap	grasp	straw
digest	flourish	perimeter	traverse
dilapidated	furrow	ploughed	unrelenting
dungarees	gadget	pumpkin	wager
field	gesture	scarecrow	

Picture quiz – weather

A Unscramble the words below and match them to the pictures.

1   2   3

4   5   6

NAIR DUCLO HUNINESS WONS
ELAG STRUNDERMOTH

1 _____   2 _____   3 _____

4 _____   5 _____   6 _____

B Which of the words below are associated with the types of weather shown above?

1 gusty ( ) **2** lightning ( ) **3** overcast ( )
4 scorching ( ) **5** downpour ( ) **6** whiteout ( )

Land of the Dragons

by Arja Faller-Nenonen

— ❧ ❧ —

Mum told us about trolls and giants, but they lived in a very faraway land. They were fairy tales. What she did not know about, but we did, were dragons. In Wales they came in all sizes. Some were so small you could not see them. How small can you get before you disappear? Some dragons were so large you could not see them. They filled the universe. We were just fleas in their scales. Then there were the normal-sized dragons, of course. They were clear to see. Take Caerphilly Mountain. That's a medium-sized dragon sleeping peacefully. It was great fun climbing to the top of its round back on a Sunday morning to look down on the town with its castle and the surrounding countryside. From there you could see the backs of other dragons curled up in their sleep. They were all waiting for a time when knights in armour would come back to give battle. Then they would wake up and fight again.

My brother and I dressed up as knights in shining armour. Mum's discarded winter boots, tunics made of sheets and curtains, cardboard helmets and wooden swords painted silver and turned into chainmail and brilliantly clashing steel. Most of the time we only frightened smaller dragons down in the old quarry at the end of our street. They fell hissing into the pond, cooled down and fell back asleep again.

Many of the valleys had lots of dragons hiding in mineshafts. They were the really mean ones. In Aberfan they even swallowed up children by sending a colliery waste tip slithering into their school. It was all in the news. We watched the devastation on the telly and our teacher told us about those poor children dying. The whole school kept a minute's silence for them.

Inside Caerphilly Castle lived some bigger dragons, too. Some of them were extremely dangerous, because they were not really asleep, only pretending. They had made a ruin of the castle and were now lurking in the corners of the dark towers and passages.

Then one day ... I could see the danger, but nobody listened when Mum suddenly got this craze about the colour midnight blue – the favourite colour of dragons. First, the kitchen cabinets, tables and chairs became midnight blue. Every day after school, we discovered something new, which had turned this colour. It was very worrying.

One day we found that the walls and ceiling of our upstairs loo on the half landing had also turned this terrifying colour of midnight blue. I told them to lock the door and bolt it from the outside. They only laughed. We never entered that loo again, but used the one downstairs which was bright primrose yellow. It was a friendly colour, but the paint was peeling and we lived in constant fear of that midnight blue paint pot. We lay awake at night worrying about the upstairs loo not being locked shut. In the end, we found a solution. We put marbles in front of the door, so we would hear when something came out and fell over them. We had a good night's sleep at last and heard nothing.

Next morning, Dad gave us a right telling off. He claimed he had nearly broken his neck slipping on the marbles. We tried to tell him it was not our fault. It was the dragon.

The move came in the summer holidays. Mum and Dad explained to us it was because Dad had got a better job in the South of England, but we knew better. It was all because of that wretched dragon in the midnight blue lavatory. But why did we have to move so far, to a place where there are no caves or mineshafts? The seaside has no wild crags or coves, only pebbles. There is not a single dragon in this land.

My brother and I dream about them still.

We will never forget the Land of the Dragons, but we know we can never return.

— ⁂ —

Words and phrases

discarded	thrown away
chainmail	type of flexible armour
hissing	making a prolonged sound like the letter 's'
mineshafts	passageways in a mine
mean	evil, nasty
colliery	coal mine
waste tip	heap of worthless material
slithering	slipping and sliding
devastation	destruction
made a ruin of	destroyed, leaving only remains standing
lurking	hiding and waiting
loo	toilet
half landing	platform halfway up a flight of stairs
marbles	small hard balls of glass
telling off	reprimand
move	relocation of home
lavatory	toilet
crags	steep rugged rocks or peaks
coves	small bays or caves
pebbles	small rounded stones

Food for thought

1. According to the narrator, what is Caerphilly Mountain?
   a. a very large dragon
   b. a medium-sized dragon
   c. a sleeping giant

2. In the story, what did the dragons do in Aberfan?
   a. They caused a disaster.
   b. They slept while a colliery waste tip destroyed a school.
   c. They tried to stop something horrible from happening.

3. Why were the children afraid of midnight blue?
   a. It made rooms seem darker and colder.
   b. They thought wet paint was dangerous.
   c. They believed it would attract dragons.

4. Why was the children's father angry with them?
   a. They had nearly caused an accident.
   b. They were always talking about dragons
   c. They didn't want to use the upstairs toilet.

5. At the end of the story, how do the children feel?
   a. They are glad that have escaped from the dragons.
   b. They like living by the seaside.
   c. They miss the place they grew up in.

Crossword puzzle

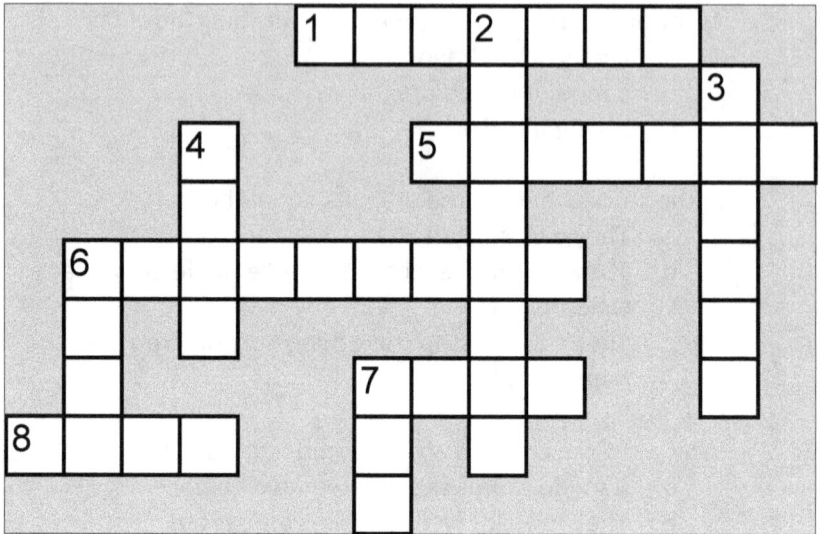

ACROSS

1 throw away
5 slip and slide
6 flexible armour
7 hide and wait
8 nasty

DOWN

2 coal mine
3 small rounded stone
4 steep rugged rock
6 small bay
7 toilet

Picture quiz – mythical beasts

A Match the words to the pictures.

1   2   3   4

5   6   7   8

CENTAUR   UNICORN   DRAGON   SATYR
CERBERUS   GORGON   FLYING HORSE   CHIMERA

1 _____ 2 _____ 3 _____ 4 _____

5 _____ 6 _____ 7 _____ 8 _____

B Match the following with the beasts above.

1 Pegasus ( ) **2** Hades ( ) **3** Smaug ( )
4 Medusa ( ) **5** Sagittarius ( ) **6** Scotland ( )
7 Grover Underwood ( ) **8** she-goat ( )

The Reunion

by Sharon Westmaas

— ❧ ❦ —

She'd surely forgotten me. After all, she hadn't seen me for thirty-five years. I was a child of ten back then and hundreds of children had since passed by. She must be over eighty now, a doddering old thing with her memory gone. But I hadn't forgotten her. So since I was in London, I picked up the phone, dialled her number, and told her who I was.

"What! No! You're here in London? Dear, I've been asking EVERYONE if they have your address. I wanted to invite you to our 60th Anniversary Reunion! You MUST come!"

No, she hadn't forgotten me. Mrs Hunter never forgets her children, and none of her children forget her. We're scattered all over the world now, but Saint Margaret's School made us members of a big happy family with her at the unifying centre.

I distinctly remember my first day, when Mummy and Daddy took me along for the interview. Mrs Hunter smiled at three-year-old me.

"You're the Three Bears, and here are the Three Chairs for you: a big chair for Daddy bear, a medium-sized chair for Mummy bear and a tiny little chair for Baby bear!"

This is a nice place, I thought, and all my fears fled.

Mrs Hunter held her school in the bottom storey of her big wooden house in Camp Street, Georgetown, British Guiana. Camp Street was a wide leafy avenue, its two lanes of traffic separated by a footpath down the middle. Huge flamboyant trees lined the walkway, sometimes covered over in brilliant red blossoms, so that I walked down a red carpet of flowers, feeling very happy and proud in my green-and-white checked uniform.

Mrs Hunter had started her school from scratch with just a handful of boys and girls. On the very next day, one of the girls brought her best friend along "because it's much nicer here," and in that vein, Saint Margaret's continued to grow over the years. It became the most sought-after primary school in the country, where even the Prime Minister sent his children – along with their bodyguards. Learning there was a process of unfolding. There was no specific time when we were told, "OK, the fun's over, now life gets serious." I started at age three and left at age ten, and along the way I learned the three R's and a lot more besides. Learning was an integral part of living, and our own natural eagerness to learn was the driving force. We played, sang, danced, acted, listened to stories, and all the time Mrs Hunter knew each child's strengths and weaknesses. Her aim was to bring out the very best in us. Her formula for excellence was simple, but it worked.

"I wanted a happy school," she told me later, "because only a happy child can learn."

Stress was unheard of, despite long hours and high standards. At midday, most of us went home for lunch and returned for afternoon school, after which there was, naturally, homework. By the time I was six, I was writing my own letters to my mother, who was living in Trinidad at the time. In my final year, I took the entrance exams for a school in England, passed easily and left Saint Margaret's for good.

I never realised how lucky I had been until it was time for my own son to start school in Germany. A tidal wave of dire warnings and grim prophecies washed over me, which I refused to believe. For me, primary school could not be anything else but a place of wonder and joy. I was very wrong.

When I sought out Mrs Hunter a couple of years ago, she was living in a tiny cramped flat in South London. Guyana had become independent and Saint Margaret's had been nationalised and turned into a government school. Mrs Hunter had been given the choice of staying on as an employee at her own beloved school, or retiring. She chose retirement, receiving a pension of about three pounds sterling a month. Luckily she was also eligible for a small British pension.

I found a woman old in years but truly young at heart, brimming over with zest, with a mind as alert and a humour as awake as ever. Of course, she had not forgotten me. And of course, I went to the Sixty-Years Reunion. So did Marjory who had been my best friend. We screeched when we saw each other in our grown up versions, and the reminiscing began.

"I was so absolutely thick," Marjory confided, "Kippy and I used to be rivals for bottom of the class. But Mrs Hunter always encouraged us."

Marjory is now a very gifted and successful artist.

The room was packed – lots of familiar faces, and lots more unfamiliar ones, all ex-pupils of Mrs Hunter who had ended up in England. There were speeches, tears, laughter, stories, memories, songs, poems, toasts to Mrs Hunter and champagne. And belated thanks. For we all knew now how fortunate we were to have passed though Saint Margaret's.

And fortunate too, that on this one day, so many years later, we could relive the good times and feel the intervening years melt away under a teacher's understanding smile.

— ❧ ❧ —

Words and phrases

doddering	shaking, dithering
scattered	spread unevenly
unifying	uniting, bringing people together
bottom storey	ground floor
flamboyant	flame like, rich, brightly coloured
from scratch	starting with nothing
a handful	a few
in that vein	that way
sought after	desired
the three R's	Reading, (w)Riting and (a)Rithmetic
integral part of	essential to
eagerness	enthusiasm
tidal wave	flood
dire warnings	advice to beware of danger
grim prophecies	gloomy predictions
nationalised	taken over by the state
retiring	ceasing to work
pension	money paid to someone who has retired
brimming over	overflowing
zest	excitement, enjoyment
gifted	talented

Food for thought

1. When the narrator made the phone call...
    a. she knew that the teacher would invite her to a reunion.
    b. she expected Mrs Hunter to remember her.
    c. she didn't really know what to expect.

2. How did she feel on her first day at school?
    a. happy at first, then disappointed
    b. fearful at first, then happy
    c. anxious at first, then frightened

3. Mrs Hunter's school was successful because...
    a. the Prime Minister sent his children there.
    b. she made sure the children enjoyed their time there.
    c. the children went to school in the morning and in the afternoon and did a lot of homework.

4. Which sentence best describes the reunion?
    a. a time for joyful reminiscence
    b. a sequence of planned speeches and toasts
    c. a formal and nervous occasion

5. Which word best sums up the mood of the story as a whole?
    a. nostalgia
    b. remembrance
    c. reconciliation

Word search

Find the words in the grid. Words can go horizontally, vertically or diagonally in any direction. When you are done, the unused letters in the grid will spell out a <u>hidden message</u>, reading from left to right, top to bottom. There will be a few letters left over.

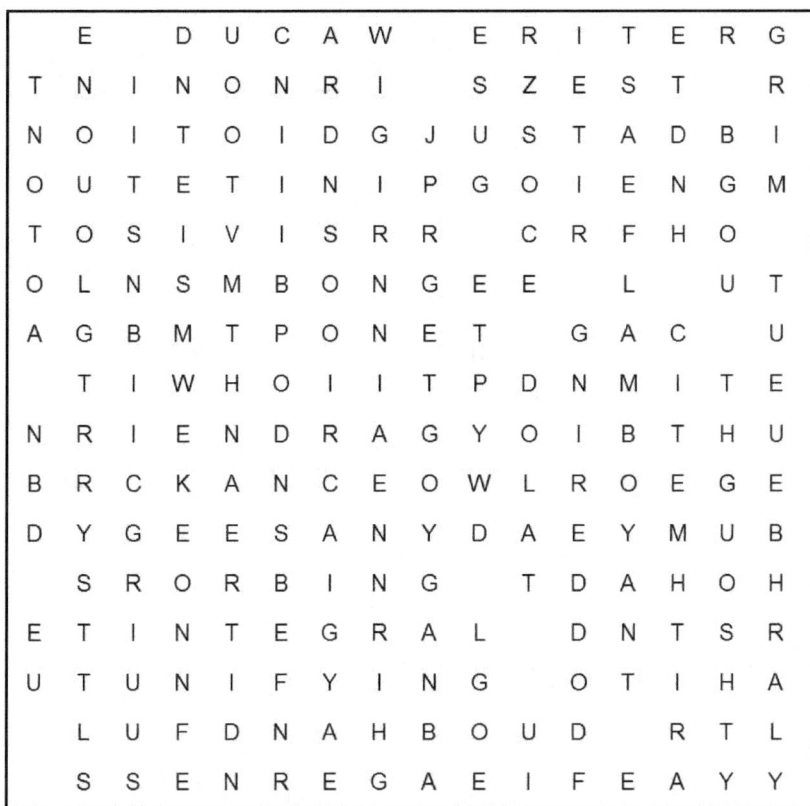

```
      E     D   U   C   A   W       E   R   I   T   E   R   G
  T   N   I   N   O   N   R   I       S   Z   E   S   T       R
  N   O   I   T   O   I   D   G   J   U   S   T   A   D   B   I
  O   U   T   E   T   I   N   I   P   G   O   I   E   N   G   M
  T   O   S   I   V   I   S   R   R       C   R   F   H   O
  O   L   N   S   M   B   O   N   G   E   E       L       U   T
  A   G   B   M   T   P   O   N   E   T       G   A   C       U
      T   I   W   H   O   I   I   T   P   D   N   M   I   T   E
  N   R   I   E   N   D   R   A   G   Y   O   I   B   T   H   U
  B   R   C   K   A   N   C   E   O   W   L   R   O   E   G   E
  D   Y   G   E   E   S   A   N   Y   D   A   E   Y   M   U   B
      S   R   O   R   B   I   N   G       T   D   A   H   O   H
  E   T   I   N   T   E   G   R   A   L       D   N   T   S   R
  U   T   U   N   I   F   Y   I   N   G       O   T   I   H   A
      L   U   F   D   N   A   H   B   O   U   D       R   T   L
      S   S   E   N   R   E   G   A   E   I   F   E   A   Y   Y
```

arithmetic	flamboyant	prophecy	storey
brimming	grim	reading	unifying
dire	handful	retire	vein
doddering	integral	scattered	writing
eagerness	pension	sought	zest

Picture quiz – school subjects

A Unscramble the school subjects below and match them to the pictures.

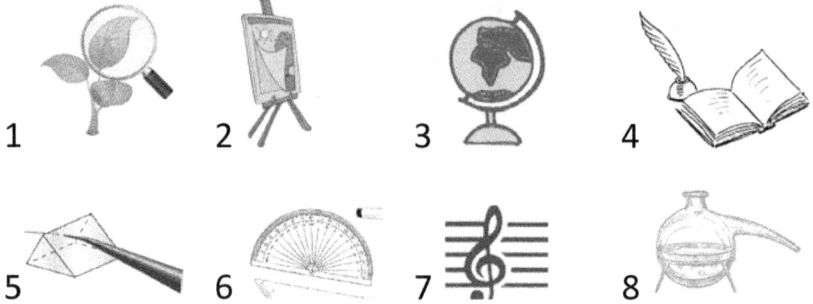

1 2 3 4

5 6 7 8

TAR   HAYPOGGER   SIPSYCH   GREYTOME
MERCYTHIS   MICUS   UTILERATER   GOBYOIL

1 _____ 2 _____ 3 _____ 4 _____

5 _____ 6 _____ 7 _____ 8 _____

B In which of the pictures above can you see the following items?

1 magnifying glass ( )   **2** quill ( )   **3** prism ( ) **4** stave ( )
5 globe ( ) **6** retort ( )   **7** protractor ( ) **8** easel ( )

The Fear

by Anthony Curtis

— ❧ ❦ —

Checking a pile of homework, Mrs Leary was interrupted by one of her pupils who had rushed into the classroom.

"Mrs Leary," he cried. "There's a bomb in the playground!"

"What are you prattling about, Timothy? What do you mean, a bomb?"

"There's a bomb in the playground," Timothy repeated.

"If this is one of your silly pranks ... I'll ... "

The teacher walked quickly out of the classroom leaving the threat unfinished, and the boy followed apprehensively.

The children in the playground looked as if they were waiting for a cue from a film director. They stood stock still in a circle staring at a boy who was lying full-length on the ground, his arms folded under his body, as if hugging something.

Mrs Leary advanced, but one of the girls said, "Don't go near him, Miss. He's sitting on a bomb."

"He's not sitting, he's lying," the teacher said, "but he can't lie there for ever."

She called to the boy. "Peter, get up, there is no sense in what you're doing. You'll not be saving any lives that way."

Peter stood up, slowly, a sickly grin on his face. The bomb now lay at his feet. It was perfectly round and rather uninteresting.

"It's a dud," said one of the children.

"Just wait until it goes off before you say that," retorted Peter.

A few of the others giggled, and Mrs Leary began to suspect a practical joke.

"Now then," she said, her voice stern, "who's responsible for this?"

"No one," said Peter, his voice dripping innocence, "at least not from our school. A man in blue overalls rolled it into the playground and shouted 'Here's a present for you.' Then he ran off."

"Is this true?"

All the children nodded their heads, and Mrs Leary, who believed emphatically that they would not collectively deceive her, felt a pang of fear.

Suddenly she realised, and it was a bit of a shock, that she had no idea what bombs really looked like. Surely they should have fins, or fuses sticking out of them. This one appeared to be so lifeless.

"All right, children. I want you to leave the playground. All of you. And quietly. Go to the old barn on the other side of Farmer Mulligan's orchard, and leave the apples where they are. In the meantime, I'll telephone the police. Now move."

The children moved. All except Timothy, who lingered behind.

"Well, Timothy, what's wrong? I'd get going if I were you."

The boy hesitated and then said, "If you please, Miss, my father's in the army. He's a bomb disposal expert."

"Oh really! And may I ask what that has to do with the present situation?"

"I thought I could try to defuse the bomb. My father showed me how."

"Young man," said Mrs Leary. "It's clear to me that you are out of your mind. If you don't get out of here right now, you'll get detention. Now move!"

Knowing the teacher could be taken at her word, Timothy moved.

Mrs Leary went to the staff room and telephoned the police. Three minutes later, there were howls of sirens and three police cars skidded into the playground. A dozen officers sprang out of the cars and formed a circle around the offending article. Nonchalantly, as if he had all the time in the world, a plainclothes policeman, who reminded Mrs Leary of her late father, walked over to her.

"Mornin' Ma'am. Bit of a problem, eh? Well, we'd better take a look – but I'd be obliged if you would stand clear. Or better still, leave the area."

"I prefer to stay," said Mrs Leary firmly.

The Inspector shrugged, "As you wish."

Then he walked over to the police-ringed bomb and surveyed it. After a minute, he bent over, took the contraption in his hands and shook it. Then, to Mrs Leary's consternation, let it fall to the ground. There was a hollow metallic clang. The bomb bounced once, rolled a few inches, wobbled, and then broke in half.

Her heart beating rapidly, Mrs Leary thought the Inspector was either a very brave man or an idiot.

"Your kids have been having you on, Ma'am," he said. "It's a fake."

Embarrassed, Mrs Leary started to apologise, but the Inspector brushed her words away with a wave of his hand and said, "I'll be off now. You can keep it as a souvenir."

When the police had gone, Mrs Leary picked the pieces up and took them into the classroom.

I'll find out who did this, she thought, savagely, even if I have to punish every single one of them.

It was then that she noticed a small slip of paper taped to the inside of one half of the bomb. Pencilled in rough characters were the words

You was lucky this time.

My children don't use grammar like that, she thought, and was proud of the fact. Something was wrong.

And she remembered what she had, up until now, deliberately cast out of her mind. Back in Belfast, all those years ago. A flat bicycle tyre had saved her life.

She had been late, and was only a hundred yards away from the school when, with a loud roar, it burst into flames. She was blown to the ground. Seconds later, debris flew over her head, and then the screams started, those of the injured mingling with her own.

Her heart pounding, Mrs Leary stared out of the window to the orchard where the children were playing.

Please let it be a practical joke … Please!

— ❧ ❧ —

Words and phrases

interrupted	stopped in the middle of something
prattling	talking or chattering foolishly
threat	warning
apprehensively	fearfully
cue	signal
stock still	not moving at all
dud	a bomb that will not explode
goes off	explodes
practical joke	prank, trick
overalls	protective working clothes
emphatically	firmly, unquestionably
pang	sudden, sharp feeling
fuses	detonation devices
barn	farm building used for storage
orchard	group of fruit trees
lingered behind	was slow to leave
defuse	make safe
detention	keeping a child in school after normal hours as a form of punishment
offending article	item of concern, dangerous object
contraption	device
consternation	alarm, fear
having you on	making a fool of you

Food for thought

1. What was Mrs Leary's initial reaction to Timothy's words?
    a. She thought someone might be playing a joke.
    b. She knew there was danger.
    c. She felt threatened.

2. What did she find in the playground?
    a. One of the children was sitting on a bomb.
    b. Peter was holding something.
    c. The children were arguing amongst themselves.

3. Why did Timothy stay behind?
    a. He wanted Mrs Leary to call his father.
    b. He was afraid to leave.
    c. He wanted to help.

4. In the inspector's opinion, who had planted the fake bomb?
    a. the children
    b. the man in blue overalls
    c. a person or persons unknown.

5. Until she saw the note, Mrs Leary...
    a. had been proud of her pupils' grammar.
    b. had decided that the children were blameless.
    c. had suppressed an unpleasant memory.

Jumbo crossword puzzle

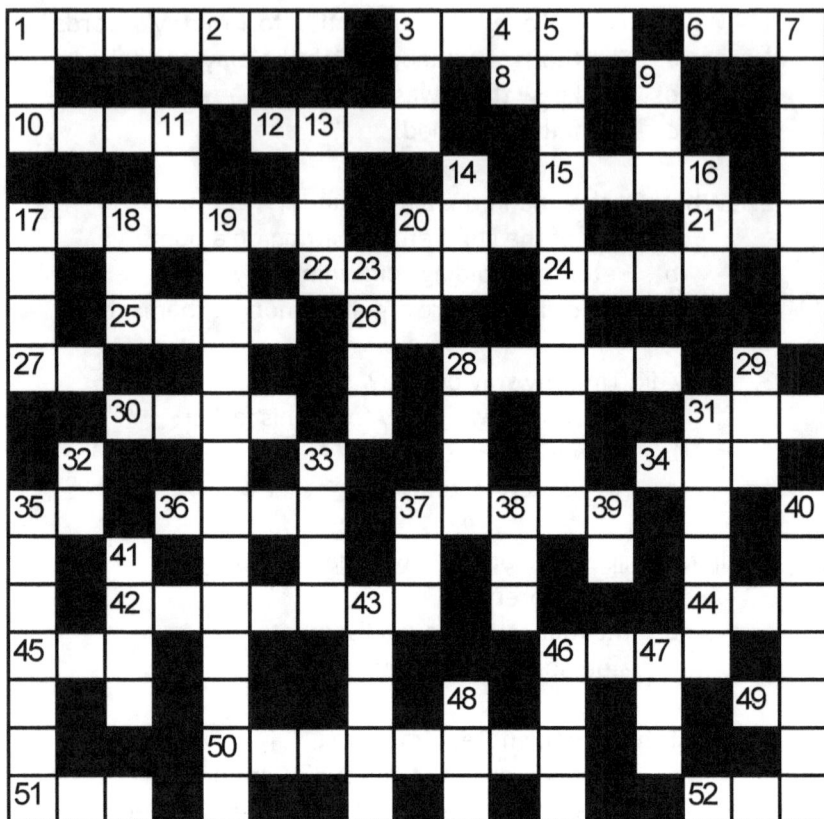

ACROSS

1 go off (bomb)
3 fix, e.g. with glue
6 also
8 *This one appeared to be ___ lifeless*
10 fighting in the streets
12 *The teacher began to suspect a practical ____*
15 armoured vehicle
17 two-wheeled vehicle
20 entrance
21 historical period
22 *With a loud ____, it burst into flames*
24 military force
25 *She felt a ____ of fear*

26 belonging to me
27 exist
28 deadly
30 major town
31 One of the children says
that the bomb is a ____
34 still, until now, nevertheless
35 ...even ____ I have to punish
every one of them
36 The inspector asks her to leave
the ____
37 metallic sound

42 chatter foolishly
44 you can ____ off a bomb
45 *My children don't ____*
grammar like that
46 The inspector says that the
bomb is a ____
49 American soldier, General
Infantry (abbr.)
50 protective clothing
51 *I'll find out who ____ this*
52 make a hole in the ground

DOWN

1 You hear with this
2 *Surely they should have fins,*
____ *fuses...*
3 feminine pronoun
4 exists
5 device
7 where the children are playing
at the end of the story
9 tin, able to
11 attempt
13 *debris flew ____ her head*
14 in favour of
16 item used to open a lock
17 explosive device
18 head wear
19 alarm, fear
20 twenty-four hour period
23 sign of something to come
28 drop down
29 however

31 Timothy offers to ____ the
bomb
32 *It's clear to me that you are*
out ____ your mind
33 If you ____ something out of
your mind you forget it
35 harmed
37 The children looked as if they
were waiting for a ____
38 put a question
39 *Don't ____ near him, Miss*
40 One of the girls said that Peter
was ____ on a bomb
41 not closed
43 Surname of the teacher in the
story
46 detonation device
47 child, young goat
48 travel through the air

Picture quiz – explosive devices

A Match the devices to the pictures.

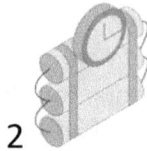

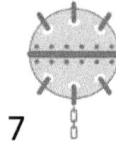

1   2   3   4

5   6   7   8

GRENADE   DYNAMITE   TIME BOMB   TORPEDO
NAVAL MINE   DOODLEBUG   PARACHUTE BOMB
DETONATOR

1 _____ 2 _____ 3 _____ 4 _____

5 _____ 6 _____ 7 _____ 8 _____

B Which of the above... ?

1 is set in advance ( ) **2** waits underwater ( )
3 was invented by Alred Nobel ( ) **4** does not
explode ( ) **5** is typically thrown by hand ( )
6 is fired from a submarine ( ) **7** has jet propusion ( )
8 is dropped from an aircraft ( )

Answer key

The Seasonal Visitor

Food for thought
1 a   **2** b   **3** c   **4** b   **5** a

Crossword puzzle

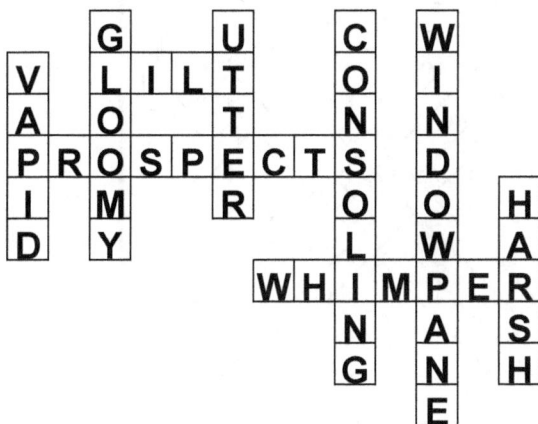

```
. . G . . U . . C . W . .
V . L I L T . . O . I . .
A . O . . T . . N . N . .
P R O S P E C T S . D . .
I . M . . R . . O . O . H
D . Y . . . . . L . W . A
. . . . . . W H I M P E R
. . . . . . . . N . A . S
. . . . . . . . G . N . H
. . . . . . . . . . E . .
```

Picture quiz

A
1 CHRISTMAS   **2** HANNUKAH   **3** EASTER   **4** HALLOWEEN
5 NEW YEAR'S EVE   **6** DIWALI / DEEPAVALI

B
1 (3)   **2** (5)   **3** (2)   **4** (6)   **5** (4)   **6** (1)

A Scarecrow in Winter

Food for thought
1 a **2** c **3** b **4** a **5** c

Word search

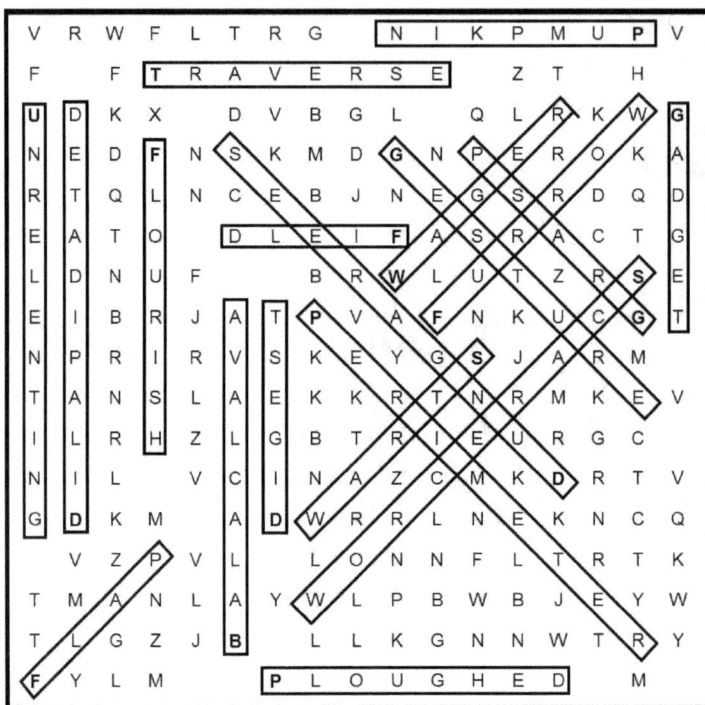

Picture quiz
A
1 SUNSHINE **2** THUNDERSTORM **3** SNOW
4 CLOUD **5** GALE **6** RAIN

B
1 (5) **2** (2) **3** (4) **4** (1) **5** (6) **6** (3)

Land of the Dragons

Food for thought
1 b **2** a **3** c **4** a **5** c

Crossword puzzle

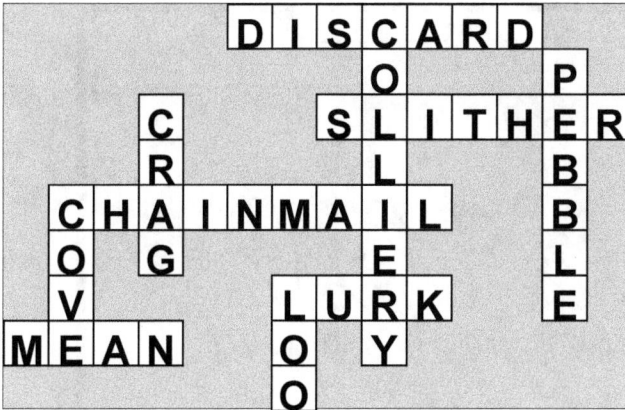

```
        D I S C A R D
              O       P
        C   S L I T H E R
        R     L       B
  C H A I N M A I L   B
  O   G       E       L
  V       L U R K     E
M E A N   O   Y
          O
```

Picture quiz
A
1 DRAGON **2** CHIMERA **3** CENTAUR **4** CERBERUS
5 UNICORN **6** SATYR **7** GORGON **8** FLYING HORSE

B
1 (8) **2** (4) **3** (1) **4** (7) **5** (3) **6** (5) **7** (6) **8** (2)

The Reunion

Food for thought
1 c   **2** b   **3** b   **4** a   **5** a

Word search

Hidden message: *'Education is not just about going to school but about widening your knowledge and absorbing the truth about life.'* – Shakuntala Devi (1929 – 2013), Indian writer whose ability to do mental arithmetic earned her a place in the Guinness Book of World Records.

Picture quiz

A

1 BIOLOGY   **2** ART   **3** GEOGRAPHY   **4** LITERATURE
5 PHYSICS   **6** GEOMETRY   **7** MUSIC   **8** CHEMISTRY

B

1 (1)   **2** (4)   **3** (5)   **4** (7)   **5** (3)   **6** (8)   **7** (6)   **8** (2)

The Fear

Food for thought

1 a **2** b **3** c **4** a **5** c

Jumbo crossword puzzle

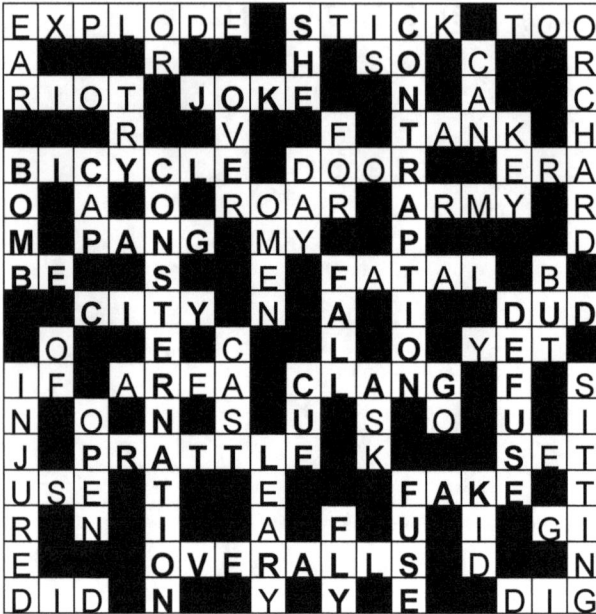

Picture quiz

A

1 DYNAMITE **2** TIME BOMB **3** PARACHUTE BOMB
4 DOODLEBUG **5** GRENADE **6** DETONATOR
7 NAVAL MINE **8** TORPEDO

B

1 (2) **2** (7) **3** (1) **4** (6) **5** (5) **6** (8) **7** (4) **8** (3)

Further titles from LinguaBooks

IN A STRANGE LAND
Short Stories for Creative Learning
Andrzej Cirocki and Alicia Peña Calvo   ISBN 978-3734789465

IN A STRANGE LAND is a collection of four original short stories which provide teachers with motivating and engaging classroom material at the CEFR B2 to C1 level and young adult learners with thought-provoking narratives and characters to whom they can relate.

This gripping teenage fiction encourages readers to use their imagination and interact with the texts in a variety of educational and experimental ways.

The stories are supported by creative tasks which enable students to integrate their various language skills, exploit computer technology, practise learning strategies and exercise autonomy.

Audio recordings of the stories are available on two separate CDs which are suitable for classroom use and can also be listened to for pleasure.

Academic Presenting and Presentations
A preparation course for university students
Peter Levrai and Averil Bolster   ISBN 978-3734783678

This practical training course is designed to help students cultivate academic presentation skills and deal with the variety of presentation tasks they may need to master during their studies.

The material is suitable for a global audience and can be used in a wide range of academic contexts since the content not only helps learners develop their presentation skills in English but also considers wider topics relevant to English for Academic Purposes, such as principles of research and the risk of plagiarism.

The accompanying online video presentations enable learners to immerse themselves still further in the material presented and witness first-hand the impact of the techniques illustrated.

A separate Teacher's Book is also available: ISBN: 978-3741242090

Developing Learner Autonomy Through Tasks
Theory, Research, Practice
Andrzej Cirocki ISBN 978-1-911369-01-1

At the heart of this study is the fostering of learner autonomy in the language classroom, in particular how learner autonomy can be developed through pedagogical tasks. The work focuses on four different approaches: learner-related, classroom-related, resource-related and technology-related.

Developing Learner Autonomy through Tasks combines classroom theory, research and practice, all of which are immersed in the philosophy of social constructivism, whereby knowledge and learning are seen as both the context for and the result of human interaction.

"This is the book everyone in the field has been waiting for. It is the product of excellent classroom research... highly engaging, relevant, readable, and above all, practical in its handling of the issues."
- Prof. John McRae, University of Nottingham, UK

Controversies in ELT
What you always wanted to know about teaching English
but were afraid to ask
Maurice Claypole ISBN 978-1-911369-00-4

This thought-provoking and informative collection of essays covers a broad spectrum of topics relating to English language teaching, including chapters on The Death Of the Communicative Approach, Teaching the Language of Sex and Teaching English in Second Life.

Also released for the first time in book form are chapters on the author's unique insight into the correlation between language, set theory and fractal mathematics - and the consequences for English teachers.

"This book provides a refreshing look at old concepts, opens our eyes to new perspectives and encourages teachers to venture along new paths."
- Elke Schulth, ELTAS, Germany

"Interesting... instructive and - not least - fun to read. A brilliant book!"
- Nick Michelioudakis, TESOL Greece